YOUR GOLDEN EARS

FIRST
PIANO
LESSONS

FOR ADULT BEGINNERS

YOUR GOLDEN EARS

FIRST PIANO LESSONS

FOR ADULT BEGINNERS

Learn With 5 Minutes Daily Practice, Master Finger Dexterity & Technique Using Sheet Music, Songs, Music Notation and More!

VOL.2

MUSIC MOUSE STUDIOS

ISBN: 978-1-962052-01-6

Contents

Introduction

Mr. Reynolds, a seasoned gentleman whose weathered hands tell stories of years gone by, sits before a piano in his home, a symbol of both his aspirations and apprehensions. As Mr. Reynolds gazes at the piano keys, a whirlwind of thoughts dances behind his eyes. The passage of time has a way of casting shadows of doubt, making the prospect of learning seem like an uphill climb. With cautious determination, Mr. Reynolds lowers his hands onto the piano keys. The initial touch is hesitant, but as his fingers find their place, a melody emerges that echoes his journey. The notes are slow, but with each one played, Mr. Reynolds discovers a renewed sense of purpose, a reminder that it's never too late to embrace a new challenge. Through perseverance, the seemingly insurmountable obstacles begin to crumble. The slow pace of learning transforms into a steady rhythm of progress. The fear that once held him captive fades into the background, replaced by the sound of newfound confidence.

As the final notes resonate in the air, Mr. Reynolds lifts his gaze from the keys. A subtle smile graces his lips, a testament to the journey he has undertaken. The piano, once an enigma, has become a canvas for his expression.

Mr. Reynolds' journey mirrors that of countless others at a similar juncture. It was as if time had unraveled, revealing the uncertainties that accompany every learner, especially growing older. The weight of years and the fear of the unfamiliar can make the pace of learning feel slower. It's a reality we all share, the tinge of intimidation when we confront the unknown.

But just as Volume 1 showed us, the beauty lies in overcoming those very challenges. We've uncovered the tools to choose the right instrument, navigate the keyboard, and decipher the enigma of musical notation. Now, with Volume 2, we're equipped to venture further. We'll master strategies to strengthen finger dexterity through both exercises and songs, deepen our understanding of harmonic analysis and major scales, and explore techniques to enhance musical expression.

With this step-by-step comprehensive piano course accompanied by online demonstration videos, you can learn in digestible 5 to 30-minute lessons how to read music from well-known classical piano literature, develop finger dexterity and flexibility, gain a deep understanding of music theory, and uncover fascinating insights about the composers and songs you're learning. Written by a music veteran, Andrea Chang, the founder of Music Mouse Studios, Andrea has a dual B.A. in Music Education and Music Composition from the University of California, Los Angeles, and is an alumni of USC's prestigious Scoring for Motion Pictures and Television program. She also is a graduate of the Conservatory of Recording Arts and Sciences. Andrea has composed music and sound design, and led audio teams for video games for over a decade. She has worked on staff at Electronic Arts, Microsoft, and Hi-Rez Studios.

So, as our pianos await, let's embark on this next chapter and rewrite the narrative together. Like with any new skill, learning the piano takes time, practice, and patience. If you don't grasp it immediately, don't be discouraged - keep practicing, and you'll get there. Your unique journey deserves to be celebrated, your dreams to be nurtured. If you wish to receive further support, please visit out our website www.musicmousestudios.com for additional resources; we have a piano YouTube channel providing demonstrations and options to receive individual support. Thank you for entrusting us with your musical education - we can't wait to walk alongside you on your piano journey!

Your Free Gift!

As a token of appreciation for your support, we would like to offer you a special gift. We have curated a collection of songs and sheet music for you to explore and enjoy, featuring a variety of songs that will further enhance your piano repertoire as you continue your piano journey after the final lesson.

To receive this exclusive free download, simply visit https://www.musicmousestudios. com/contact and include the text "SHEET MUSIC" in your message. We hope these musical gems will bring you joy and inspiration. Thank you for choosing our book!

Join Our Community!

The joy of learning the piano is even greater when shared with a community of like-minded individuals. We would like to invite you to join our piano community, where you can connect with fellow pianists, share your experiences, and receive support along your musical path. Engage in inspiring conversations, exchange tips and techniques, and discover new insights from others who are on the same piano journey as you. Together, we can celebrate achievements, overcome challenges, and foster a sense of camaraderie in our shared passion for music.

To become a part of our community,
visit our website at https://www.musicmousestudios.com/community
and join us today!

Pacing

Each lesson is small, digestible, and designed to be completed within, on average, a 5-30 minute timeframe (though some lessons may take longer). If you need to review a lesson from a previous day, we encourage you to do so – repetition is key to reinforcing and solidifying your understanding of the material. If you already have some musical background, feel free to complete more than one lesson a day. This book is intended to be adaptable to learners starting at various "beginner" levels.

The goal is for each lesson to feel like a one-on-one session with a teacher, so some material will be repeated to help review and build upon the concepts you've learned from previous lessons.

Before diving into each lesson, make sure to scan the QR code below to access the accompanying instructional videos or visit https://www.musicmousestudios.com/ piano-instructional-videos. These videos will provide invaluable guidance and enhance your learning experience. So without further ado, let's get started!

LESSON
13
Focusing on Finger Dexerity

In this lesson, we will focus on strengthening our finger dexterity as we learn how to play arpeggios in our warm-ups and new song! Let's dive in!

Arpeggios

We're going to learn how to play some arpeggios. Arpeggios consist of breaking up a chord and playing the individual notes sequentially (or "arpeggiated").

As a refresher, to form a triad (a 3-note chord), we need the 1, 3, and 5 notes of that scale.

Label the 1, 3, and 5 with the following starting notes.

1 C
    1 ____
    3 ____
    5 ____

2 G
    1 ____
    3 ____
    5 ____

3 F
    1 ____
    3 ____
    5 ____

For C (Major), the 1, 3, and 5 are C, E, and G, respectively.
For G (Major), the 1, 3, and 5 are G, B, and D, respectively.
For F (Major), the 1, 3, and 5 are F, A, and C, respectively.

First, we will play a C Major arpeggio with our left hand. Notice that it is in 3/4, meaning there are 3 beats in a measure, and the quarter note gets the beat.

☐ Write the letters below each of the notes.

☐ Play the arpeggio with the fingering provided.

Video link: https://www.musicmousestudios.com/piano-instructional-videos

Next, we will play a G Major arpeggio with our left hand.

☐ Write the letters below each of the notes.

☐ Play the arpeggio with the fingering provided.

Lastly, we will play an F Major arpeggio with our left hand.

☐ Write the letters below each of the notes.

☐ Play the arpeggio with the fingering provided.

Now that we can play these left hand arpeggios, our next song will be a breeze!

Tempo Markings

Here are some common tempo markings you should familiarize yourself with ("bpm" or "beats per a measure" is the same as "quarter note ="):

At the beginning of a piece, there is typically a tempo indication in the upper left of the music score. This guides the performer on the speed at which the song should be played. In "Brahm's Lullaby" (as seen in the score below), we observe the tempo marking "Andante" alongside a quarter note value of 100. "Andante" signifies a moderate, walking tempo. The quarter note = 100 indicates to set your metronome at 100 to play this piece.

Below are some frequently encountered tempo markings with their approximate metronome settings (notated in "bpm" or "beats per minute").

Larghissimo = "Very, very slowly," 20 bpm or less

Grave = "Slowly, solemnly," 20-40 bpm

Largo / Lento = "Very Slowly," 40-60 bpm

Adagio = "Slowly," 60-70 bpm

Adante = "At a Walking Pace," 70-100bpm

Moderato = "Moderately," 100-120bpm

Allegro = "Fast," 120-170bpm

Presto = "Very Fast," 170-200bpm

Prestissimo = "Extremely Fast," 200bpm+

Dynamics

Other markings you'll frequently encounter in music are dynamics, which instruct the performer on the volume at which to play the piece. In "Brahm's Lullaby," you will notice several dynamic markings such as *p, mf, f, and mp*.

The *p* stands for "piano," indicating to play "softly."

The *mp* stands for "mezzo-piano." "Mezzo" in Italian means "middle" or "half," implying one should play medium softly or slightly louder than *piano.*

The *f* stands for "forte," signifying to play loudly. In Italian, "forte" translates to "strong."

Similar to *mp*, *mf* stands for "mezzo-forte," instructing the performer to play "medium loud."

There are two additional markings not present in the piece but good to know.

If you come across **pp**, it stands for pianissimo, which means playing very quietly.

Conversely, **ff** denotes fortissimo, indicating to play very loudly! The suffix "issimo" in Italian serves as a superlative that means "very" or "extremely."

You may also encounter sideways "V" shaped lines resembling hairpins within the music. These are crescendo and decrescendo markings. A **crescendo** signifies a gradual increase in volume, while a **decrescendo** indicates a gradual decrease in volume.

crescendo   decrescendo

In summary,

ff = fortissimo, play very loudly

f = forte, play loudly

mf = mezzo forte, play medium loudly

mp = mezzo piano, play medium softly

p = piano, play softly

pp = pianissimo, play very softly

crescendo = gradually play louder

decrescendo = gradually play softer

New Song: "Brahms Lullaby"

☐ Write down all the letters above or below the music notes.

☐ Circle the time signature of the song. How many beats are in a measure? Which note gets the beat?

☐ Circle all the dynamics you see in the song.

Where do you play softly?

Where do you play loudly?

Where do you play medium soft?

Where do you play medium loud?

Where do you crescendo? Where do you decrescendo?

Brahm's Lullaby
for Piano

Johannes Brahms
Arranged by Andrea Chang

☐ Clap and count the rhythm of the right hand.

☐ Clap and count the rhythm of the left hand.

☐ Finger the right hand on the table. Follow the fingering provided.

☐ Finger the left hand on the table. Follow the fingering provided. Notice how these are the same arpeggios we played earlier.

☐ Finger the song with both hands on the table.

☐ Play this song slowly with your left hand first.

☐ Play this song slowly with your right hand.

☐ Play this song slowly with hands together. OPTIONAL: You can speed it up once you have mastered it.

Video link: *https://www.musicmousestudios.com/piano-instructional-videos*

About Johannes Brahms

Johannes Brahms was an acclaimed German composer who lived from 1833 to 1897. His compositions for orchestra, piano, voice, choir, and chamber ensembles were instrumental in defining the Romantic period music aesthetic. Initially taught by his father, Brahms displayed exceptional talent as a virtuosic pianist. At age 10, he gave his first concert, showcasing works by Beethoven and Mozart. While Brahms' family hoped he would focus on becoming a performer, to their dismay, Brahms invested much of his energy in composing. Brahms adopted the pseudonym "G. W. Marks" to conceal his identity and often wanted to destroy his earlier works, as he was very self-critical and a perfectionist.

During his career, Brahms collaborated with esteemed musicians of his time, such as the pianist Clara Schumann (wife of composer Robert Schumann) and the greatest violinist of their day, Joseph Joachim, who introduced Brahms to the Schumanns. At the age of 20, Brahms arrived at the Schumanns' doorstep, presenting Joachim's letter of recommendation to Robert Schumann. Schumann invited Brahms to play some of his works for him and was so impressed by Brahms that he published an article in his music magazine, *Neue Zeitschrift für Musik*, praising Brahms and said he was "fated to give expression to the times in the highest and most ideal manner." Brahms was overwhelmed with gratitude for the love and kindness Schumann showed him.

Schumann warmly welcomed Brahms into his home and mentored him. Unfortunately, Robert Schumann's mental health deteriorated, leading him to attempt suicide by jumping off a bridge. Though he was saved, he was subsequently confined to a psychiatric institution, where he spent the remainder of his days and ultimately died of pneumonia two years later.

Clara Schumann, Robert's wife, was prohibited from seeing him, so Brahms acted as an intermediary between the two and assisted Clara with household affairs. Brahms harbored a deep affection for Clara throughout her life, and they exchanged numerous letters over the years but never consummated their love. However, the true nature of their relationship remains unknown, as Brahms urged Clara to destroy his letters. In dedication to Clara, Brahms composed his Op. 9, the *Variations on a Theme of Schumann*.

"Brahms' Lullaby," also known as the "Cradle Song," was written for Brahms' friend Bertha Faber. Brahms first met Bertha when she sang in his women's choir in Hamburg. Although Brahms had feelings for her in her youth, they lost touch until he relocated to Vienna. By then, Bertha was married and expecting her second child, to whom Brahms composed this lullaby for. The melody originated from a Viennese song that Bertha used to sing to Brahms. Brahms wrote to Bertha's husband, stating, "Frau Bertha will realize that I wrote the 'Wiegenlied' for her little one. She will find it quite in order... that while she is singing Hans to sleep, a love song is being sung to her." The song was initially performed by Luise Dustmann on vocals, accompanied by Clara Schumann on piano.

☐ Perform "Brahms Lullaby" for someone or share it with us on our website www.music-mousestudios.com!

Congratulations, you've completed Lesson 13!

"Believe me, my journey has not been a simple journey of progress. There have been many ups and downs, and it is the choices that I made at each of those times that have helped shape what I have achieved."

—SATYA NADELLA, CEO
AND CHAIRMAN OF MICROSOFT

LESSON
14
Captivating Cadences

Our next lesson is dedicated to exploring the different ways in which music phrases or songs can come to an end. We will delve into the fascinating concept of open-ended versus closed musical cadences, which are crafted through the interplay and push and pull of various harmonies!

Warmup Review

☐ Play a C Major Scale with both hands ascending and descending 5 times.

☐ Play the following arpeggios in C, G, and F Major with your left hand.

☐ With your right hand, play these arpeggios in C, G, and F Major:

Video link: https://www.musicmousestudios.com/piano-instructional-videos

Chord Progressions I IV, V, VI

In the key of C Major, the scale's 1st, 4th, and 5th letters are C, F, and G, respectively. The 1, 4, and 5 chords, also known as I, IV, and V using Roman numerals, play a significant role in building harmonies in music. **Harmony** refers to the sequence of chords played in succession in a song. During our warm-up, we played the C, F, and G arpeggios, which, in the key of C Major, correspond to the harmonic progression of I, IV, and V.

Today, we will explore a new song called "Danny Boy," also in C Major, which utilizes the I, IV, and V chords. Additionally, it introduces a new chord, the vi (6th) chord, on A.

Each of these Roman Numeral chords has its own name. The I chord is known as the "**tonic**," the IV chord as the "**subdominant**," and the V chord as the "**dominant**." The tonic establishes the key and acts as a home base chord that the song consistently returns to. The dominant is important because it drives the harmonic progression back to the tonic. In "Danny Boy," the new chord, vi, is called the "**submediant**." The prefix "sub" means "below" or "what comes before," similar to a "subway," which is underground. Therefore, the sub-dominant (IV) comes *before* the dominant (V).

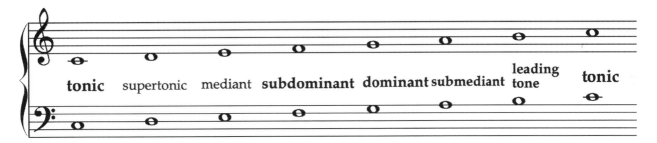

The remaining notes in the scale also have their corresponding Roman Numerals and names. The prefix "super" denotes "above," as seen in the word "superior." Hence, the "**supertonic**," which is the ii chord, is positioned "above" the tonic (I chord). The iii chord is called the "**mediant**." "Mediant" refers to the "middle" since it sits in the middle of the tonic and dominant. Similarly, the submediant, or the "lower mediant," is halfway between the dominant and leading tone, giving it its name. The vii chord, known as the "**leading tone**," leads the listener's ear back to resolution at the tonic. Familiarize yourself with these chords in the C Major scale above.

"Danny Boy" Harmonic Analysis

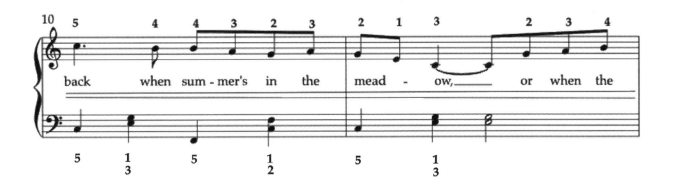

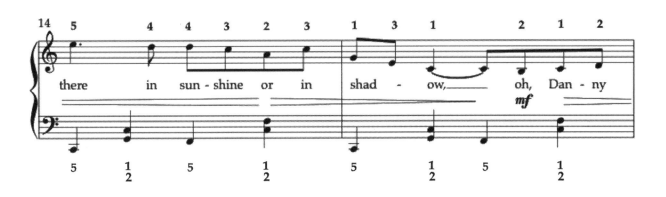

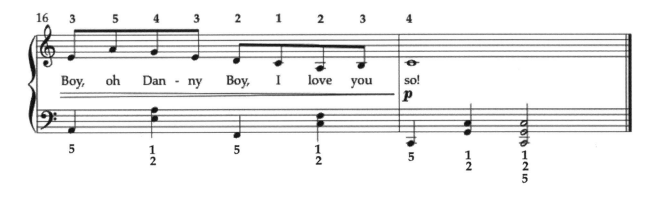

Identify and Play it!

1 Look at the left hand in the 2nd measure.
  a What notes are they?
  b What chord does this make?
  c What Roman numeral are they on the scale?
  d What is the name given for that Roman Numeral?
  e Use the fingering provided in the song to play these left hand chords

Video link: https://www.musicmousestudios.com/piano-instructional-videos

***Answers are in the section below.*

2 Look at the left hand in the 3rd measure.
  a What notes are they?
  b What chord does this make?
  c What Roman numeral are they on the scale?
  d What is the name given for that Roman Numeral?
  e Use the fingering in the song to play these left hand chords.

3 Look at the left hand in the 4th measure.
  a What notes are they?
  b What chord does this make?
  c What Roman numeral are they on the scale?
  d What is the name given for that Roman Numeral?
  e Use the fingering in the song to play these left hand chords.

4 Look at the left hand in the 5th measure.
  a What notes are they?
  b What chord does this make?
  c What Roman numeral are they on the scale?
  d What is the name given for that Roman Numeral?
  e Use the fingering in the song to play these left hand chords.

5 Look at the left hand in the 6th measure.
  a What notes are they?
  b What chord does this make?
  c What Roman numeral are they on the scale?
  d What is the name given for that Roman Numeral?
  e Use the fingering in the song to play these left hand chords.

6 Look at the left hand in the 7th measure.
  a What notes are they?
  b What chord does this make?
  c What Roman numeral are they on the scale?
  d What is the name given for that Roman Numeral?
  e Use the fingering in the song to play these left hand chords.

7 Look at the left hand in the 8th measure.

   a What notes are they?

   b What chords do they make?

   c What Roman numeral are they on the scale?

   d What is the name given for that Roman Numeral?

   e Use the fingering provided in the song to play these left hand chords.

8 Look at the left hand in the 9th measure.

   a What notes are they?

   b What chord does this make?

   c What Roman numeral are they on the scale?

   d What is the name given for that Roman Numeral?

   e Use the fingering in the song to play these left hand chords.

9 Look at the left hand in the 10th measure.

   a What notes are they?

   b What chords do they make?

   c What Roman numeral are they on the scale?

   d What is the name given for that Roman Numeral?

   e Use the fingering in the song to play these left hand chords.

10 Look at the left hand in the 11th measure.

    a What notes are they?

    b What chord does this make?

    c What Roman numeral are they on the scale?

    d What is the name given for that Roman Numeral?

    e Use the fingering provided in the song to play these left hand chords.

11 Look at the left hand in the 12th measure.

    a What notes are they?

    b What chords do they make?

    c What Roman numeral are they on the scale?

    d What is the name given for that Roman Numeral?

    e Use the fingering provided in the song to play these left hand chords.

12 Look at the left hand in the 13th measure.

    a What notes are they?

    b What chord does this make?

    c What Roman numeral are they on the scale?

    d What is the name given for that Roman Numeral?

    e Use the fingering in the song to play these left hand chords.

13 Look at the left hand in the 14th and 15th measures.
   a What notes are they?
   b What chord does this make?
   c What Roman numeral are they on the scale?
   d What is the name given for that Roman Numeral?
   e Use the fingering in the song to play these left hand chords.

14 Look at the left hand in the 16th measure.
   a What notes are they?
   b What chords do they make?
   c What Roman numeral are they on the scale?
   d What is the name given for that Roman Numeral?
   e Use the fingering in the song to play these left hand chords.

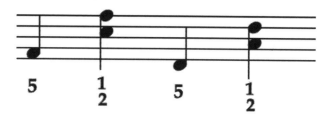

15 Look at the left hand in the 17th measure.
   a What notes are they?
   b What chord does this make?
   c What Roman numeral are they on the scale?
   d What is the name given for that Roman Numeral?
   e Use the fingering provided in the song to play these left hand chords.

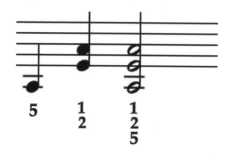

Answers

1   **a**   C, E G, E G
     b   C Major
     c   I
     d   Tonic

2   **a**   F, C F, C F
     b   F Major
     c   IV
     d   Subdominant

3   **a**   C, E G, E G
     b   C Major
     c   I
     d   Tonic

4   **a**   G, D G, D G
     b   G Major
     c   V
     d   Dominant

5   **a**   C, E G, E G
     b   C Major
     c   I
     d   Tonic

6   **a**   F, C F, C F
     b   F Major
     c   IV
     d   Subdominant

7   **a**   C, E G, and G, D G
     b   C Major, G Major
     c   I, V,
     d   Tonic, Dominant

8   **a**   C, E G, E G
     b   C Major
     c   I
     d   Tonic

9   **a**   C, E G, and F, C F
     b   C Major, F Major
     c   I, IV
     d   Tonic, Subdominant

10   **a**   C, E G, E G
     b   C Major
     c   I
     d   Tonic

11   **a**   A, E A, and F, C F
     b   A minor (we will go over this in a later lesson, so don't worry about fully understanding this at the moment), F Major
     c   vi, IV
     d   Submediant, Subdominant

12   **a**   G, D G, D G, D G
     b   G Major
     c   V
     d   Dominant

13   **a**   C, G C and F, C F
     b   C Major, F Major
     c   I, IV
     d   Tonic, Subdominant

14   **a**   A, E A, and F, C F
     b   A minor, F Major
     c   vi, IV
     d   submediant, subdominant

15   **a**   C, G C, C G C
     b   C Major
     c   I
     d   tonic

Authentic, Plagal, Half Cadences

Having identified all the chords in the song, we can see that the harmonic progression is organized into 2-measure long melodic phrases. Here is the harmonic progression for "Danny Boy," separated into rows for clarity:

Row 1: I, IV

Row 2: I, V

Row 3: I, IV

Row 4: I, V, I

Row 5: I IV, I

Row 6: vi, IV, V

Row 7: I, IV, I, IV

Row 8: vi, IV, I

The I, IV, and V chords are prevalent in this song's harmony. We also see patterns in the endings of the phrases, such as I IV, V I, I V I, or vi IV V. These phrase endings are called **cadences**. Here are several common cadences:

Authentic Cadence – V I
Plagal Cadence – IV I
Half Cadence – I V

An **Authentic Cadence** concludes a musical phrase by resolving from the **dominant (V) to the tonic (I).** A **Plagal Cadence** achieves a similar resolution by moving from the **subdominant (IV) back to the tonic (I).** A **Half Cadence**, on the other hand, does not resolve to the tonic (I) but instead leaves it unresolved on an **open-ended note with the dominant (V).** Here are some examples in our piece, "Danny Boy," where we can see some examples of Authentic, Plagal, and Half Cadences.

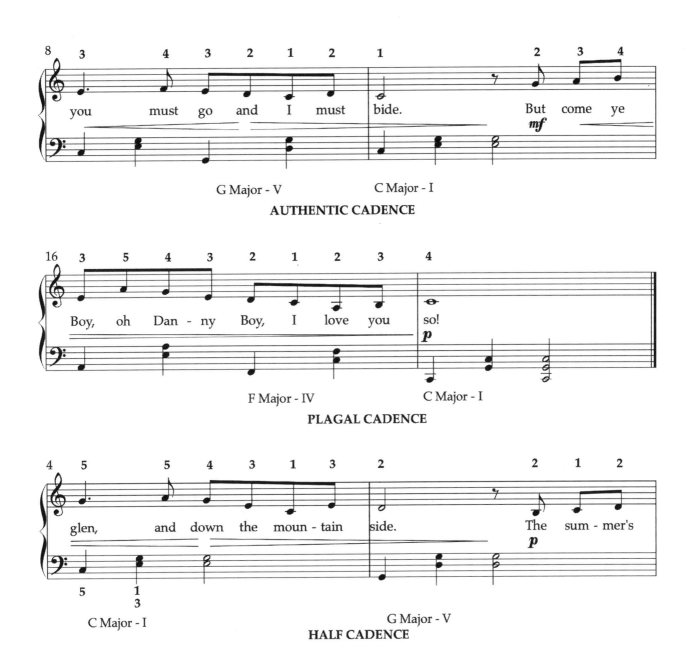

Video link: https://www.musicmousestudios.com/piano-instructional-videos

New Song: "Danny Boy"

Danny Boy
for Piano

Traditional Irish Melody
Arranged by Andrea Chang

Lento ♩=55

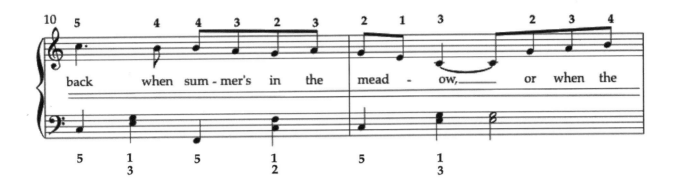

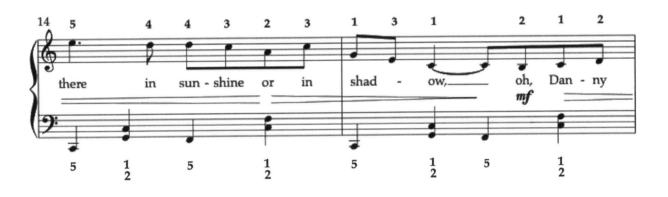

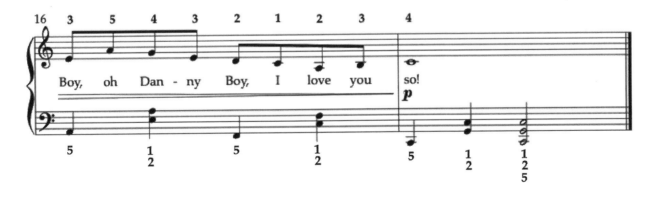

Now that we know the harmonic progression of "Danny Boy," let's try playing it.

☐ Write down all the letters above the music notes.

☐ Circle all the plagal cadences.

☐ Draw a rectangle around all the authentic cadences.

☐ Draw a triangle around all the half cadences.

☐ What is the time signature of the song?

How many beats are in a measure? Which note gets the beat?

☐ What dynamics do you see in the song?

Where do you play softly?

Where do you play loudly?

Where do you play medium soft?

Where do you play medium loud?

Where do you crescendo?

Where do you decrescendo?

☐ What is the starting tempo of the song? Lento means "slowly." What number should you set your metronome to?

Video link: https://www.musicmousestudios.com/piano-instructional-videos

☐ Clap and count the rhythm of the right hand.

☐ Clap and count the rhythm of the left hand.

☐ Finger the right hand on the table. Follow the fingering provided in the song.

☐ Finger the left hand on the table.

☐ Finger the song with both hands on the table.

☐ Play this song slowly with your left hand first.

☐ Play this song slowly with your right hand.

☐ Play this song slowly at quarter note =55 with hands together.

Congratulations, you've completed Lesson 14!

"No matter how many mistakes you make or how slow you progress, you are still way ahead of everyone who isn't trying."

—TONY ROBBINS

LESSON
15
Stepping It Up

In the next lesson, we'll explore various types of piano steps and how different melodic motions affect both the piano melody as well as our finger movements!

DAY 136 Warmup Review

☐ Play a C Major Scale with both hands ascending and descending 5 times.

☐ With your left hand, play these arpeggios in C, G, and F Major:

☐ With your right hand, play these arpeggios in C, G, and F Major:

Half Steps, Sharps, Flats, Enharmonics

A **half step** is the next step up or down from the current note being played, whether it's a white key or a black key. For instance, moving from C to C# (the black key next to C) is a half step. Refer to the visual below to see all of the half steps. A **sharp** (♯) denotes a half step increase up from the current note, corresponding to moving one key to the right. Conversely, a **flat** (♭) occurs when you lower the note a half step down to the left of the note.

One important consideration is that a sharp or flat only applies for the duration of the measure (if it's not a part of the key signature, which we'll discuss further).

In most cases, a half step involves transitioning from a white note to a black note, except when moving from E to F or from B to C.

In the image below, notice how the black keys on one keyboard are labeled differently from those on the other. For instance, C♯ and D♭ are different names for the same note. This is called an **enharmonic**. Likewise, F♯ and G♭ are examples of enharmonics.

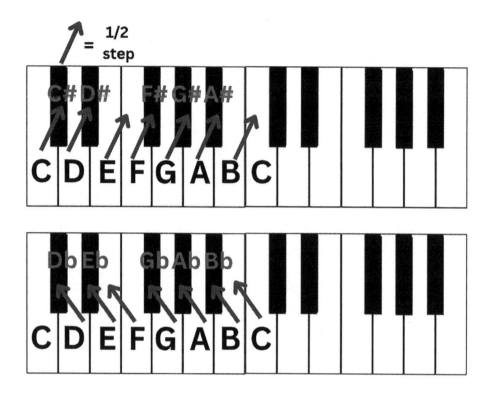

A **whole step** consists of two half steps from the current note on the piano and can be ascending or descending. The illustration below shows various examples of whole step movements on the piano. Each purple arrow represents a whole step.

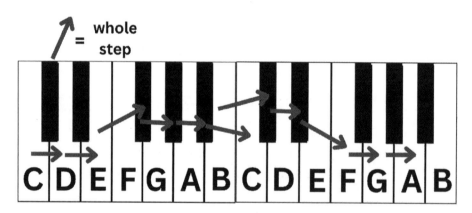

Half Step or Whole Step?

Exercise 1

☐ In the exercise below, you will ascend in the **treble clef** by half steps. Please draw the note that should follow for each note provided.

☐ In the exercise below, you will ascend in the **bass clef** by half steps. Please draw the note that should follow for each note provided.

Answers

Identify if the notes on the piano are moving in half steps or whole steps.

1

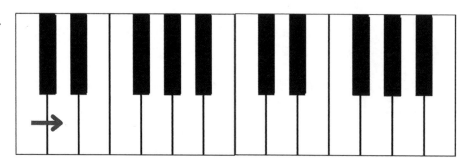

2

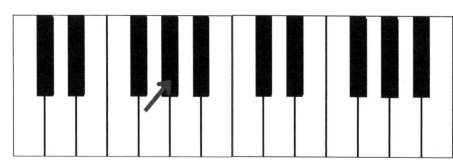

3

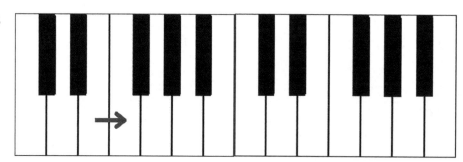

4

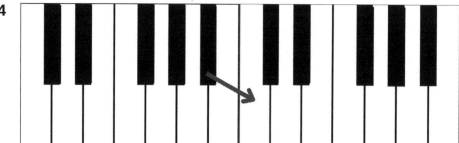

Answers

1 Whole step

2 Half step

3 Half step

4 Whole step

Exercise 3

☐ Identify if the notes below on the staff are moving in half steps or whole steps. If they are moving in half steps, fill in the blank with an "h." If they are moving in whole steps, fill in the blank with a "w."

Answers

Major Scale

A major scale follows this pattern of whole steps (w) and half steps (h):

wwh

w

wwh

or unabbreviated:

whole whole half

whole

whole whole half

Notice how the pattern consists of 2 "wwh" 's connected by a "w." This is something that you may not have realized but have already learned in previous warmups when playing a C Major scale, which follows this wwh, w, wwh pattern.

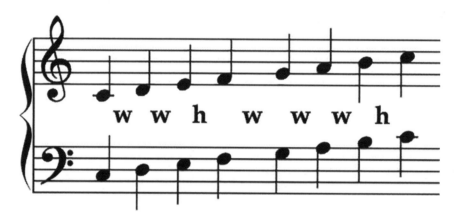

☐ Playing exercise #1: With both hands, play a C Major scale up and down **while counting the whole half pattern.**

Video link: https://www.musicmousestudios.com/piano-instructional-videos

Playing and Notation Exercises

☐ As a challenge, try playing a G Major scale using the whole half pattern.

Video link: https://www.musicmousestudios.com/piano-instructional-videos

Here is what a G Major scale looks like written on the staff with the whole half pattern. Notice how there is an F♯ written to account for the half step at the end of the pattern.

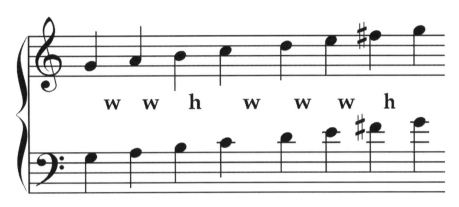

☐ Notation exercise: draw a C Major scale on the grand staff below and label all whole and half steps.

☐ Notation exercise: draw a G Major scale on the grand staff below and label all whole and half steps.

Congratulations, you've completed Lesson 15!

"You can do what you have to do, and sometimes you can do it even better than you think you can."

—JIMMY CARTER

LESSON
16
Unleashing Your Fingers

In this next lesson, we are taking it up a notch by introducing 16th notes
and applying them to a beautiful prelude composed by Bach!

16th Notes and 16th Rests

The smallest and fastest rhythmic unit we've covered in the rhythm tree so far has been 8th notes. We can extend this even further by cutting 8th notes in half, and as a result, we have 16th notes. There are four 16th notes in a beat and sixteen 16th notes in a whole note, hence its name. The same applies to cutting 8th rests in half, which results in 16th rests. Similarly, there are four 16th rests in a beat and sixteen 16th rests in a whole rest.

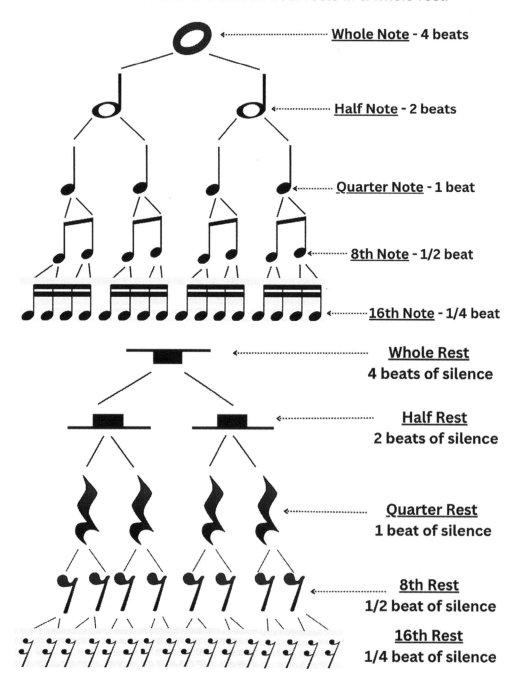

Whole Note - 4 beats

Half Note - 2 beats

Quarter Note - 1 beat

8th Note - 1/2 beat

16th Note - 1/4 beat

Whole Rest
4 beats of silence

Half Rest
2 beats of silence

Quarter Rest
1 beat of silence

8th Rest
1/2 beat of silence

16th Rest
1/4 beat of silence

To count 16th notes, it is similar to 8th notes where we have "1 & 2 &...," but we fill in the extra notes in between with an "a" and say, "one a and a."

☐ Clap through the extended rhythm tree with the 16th notes.

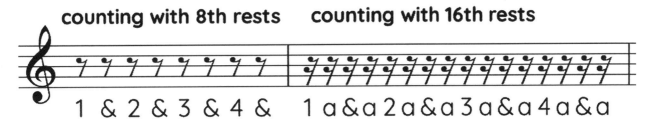

☐ "Clap" through the extended rests tree with the 16th rests.

Video link: *https://www.musicmousestudios.com/piano-instructional-videos*

DAY 143

Dotted 8th Notes

Similar to how dotted quarter notes are often followed by an 8th note, dotted 8th notes are often followed by a 16th note.

A dotted 8th note is the same as an 8th note + a 16th note, so when counting, we must allot out three 16th note beats to them.

☐ Clap and count the measure below.

Video link: https://www.musicmousestudios.com/piano-instructional-videos

Rhythm Exercises

☐ Practice Exercise #1 – Clap and count the rhythm below. Notice how we start with an 8th rest, which is the same as two 16th rests or "1a." Then we start clapping on the "&a" of the first and 3rd beats.

☐ Practice Exercise #2 – Clap and count the rhythm below. Notice how we start with a 16th note followed by a dotted 8th note, which is then tied to a quarter note. Remember that when there is a tie, you hold the note across the duration of all the notes in the tie (so you would only play on "1," "a" of 1, "3," and "a" of 3).

Video link: https://www.musicmousestudios.com/piano-instructional-videos

☐ Practice Exercise #3 – Let's take the rhythm from Exercise 1 and apply them to some notes! Play the following exercise. Write down the letter notes if needed. Please use the fingering provided. Also, note the dynamics and practice incorporating them into your playing.

> **Tip 1:** While practicing these exercises, try to rotate your wrist towards the high E every time you play it. This technique will enhance the connection between your fingers, creating smoother and more fluid movements and sounds. Keep your fingers and hands loose and allow them to flow in the direction of the notes.

> **Tip 2**: Please note that the fingering provided is merely a suggestion. If you find it more comfortable to use different fingers for certain notes, feel free to make adjustments according to your preference and ease of playing.

> *Video link*: *https://www.musicmousestudios.com/piano-instructional-videos*

Play the rest of the exercises below with the appropriate rhythm, fingering, and dynamics. Write down the letter notes if needed.

☐ Practice Exercise #4

☐ Practice Exercise #5

☐ Practice Exercise #6

☐ Practice Exercise #7

Play the rest of the exercises below with the appropriate rhythm, fingering, and dynamics. Write down the letter notes if needed.

Video link: *https://www.musicmousestudios.com/piano-instructional-videos*

☐ Practice Exercise #8

☐ Practice Exercise #9

☐ Practice Exercise #10 – **Play this with your left hand.** Notice that we hold both the C while playing the E right after it. This rhythm is the same as in Practice Exercise #2, except you hold the first note for the entire duration.

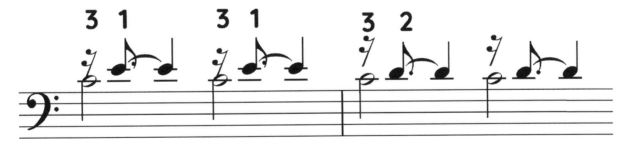

☐ Practice Exercise #11

New Song: "Prelude in C Major" (Part 1)

Most of the songs we've looked at so far have been in C Major (using all of the white keys). Though C Major doesn't naturally contain any sharps or flats, we can still have pieces in C Major that add sharps and flats in various measures, such as in Johann Sebastian Bach's "Prelude in C Major."

In this piece, the right hand plays arpeggios most of the time while the left hand keeps it steady with a bass line. You will also feel the tension, the push and pull between chords in this song, which is caused by the harmonic progression and the need for notes to resolve back to the tonic. We won't analyze the harmony here like in "Danny Boy," but that is an excellent exercise if you want a challenge!

Since this song is a bit longer, we will break it into 4 sections to learn throughout the next several lessons.

In measure 1, "*simile*" means "similar," indicating that you should play beats 3-4 in a similar way to beats 1-2. This mainly refers to using the same fingering, but if you look at the notes in beats 1-2, they are exactly the same as the notes in beats 3-4.

☐ Write down all the letters above or below the music notes.

☐ Circle all the places where you play *p*.

☐ Circle all the places where you play *f*.

☐ Circle all the places where you play *pp*.

☐ What measure do you crescendo?

☐ What measure do you decrescendo?

☐ What is the time signature of the piece? How many beats per measure are there, and what note gets the beat?

Video link: https://www.musicmousestudios.com/piano-instructional-videos

☐ Clap and count the rhythm of the right hand. Notice how every single measure has the same rhythm.

☐ Clap and count the rhythm of the left hand. Notice how every single measure has the same rhythm.

☐ Finger the right hand on the table. Follow the fingering provided.

☐ Finger the left hand on the table. Follow the fingering provided.

☐ Finger the song with both hands on the table.

☐ Play this song slowly with your right hand first.

☐ Play this song slowly with your left hand.

☐ Play this song slowly with hands together.

Prelude in C Major
from The Well-Tempered Clavier

Johann Sebastian Bach

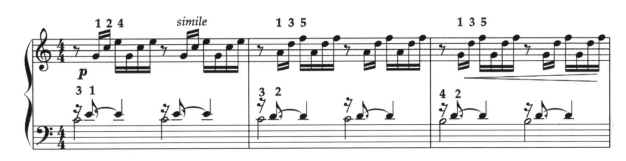

About Johann Sebastian Bach

Johannes Sebastian Bach, one of the greatest composers of all time, lived from 1685 to 1750 and wrote "Prelude in C Major." He was a German composer born into a musical family, with his father being a city musician and his eldest brother an organist. Bach was the youngest of eight children, coming from a lineage of composers. Tragically, he became an orphan at the age of 10 when both his mother and father passed away within eight months of each other. He then lived with his eldest brother, Johann Christoph Bach, who was fourteen years his senior, for 5 years.

Bach worked as a musician for Protestant churches, which influenced his compositions for organ and chamber music. He had a pattern of conflicts with authority figures, such as expressing dissatisfaction with the quality of singers in his choir and receiving a reprimand after calling one of his students a "weenie bassoonist." This student then hit Bach with a stick. Bach also faced consequences for informing his employer he would be gone for 4 weeks but instead traveled for 4 months. Bach later took on a job as a court organist but fell out of favor with his employer and ended up being dismissed and subsequently imprisoned. His discharge from jail was also unfavorable, as he too stubbornly pressed for his dismissal. However, he later received the honor of "Royal Court Composer" from the king of Poland, Augustus III.

Bach's extensive and diverse musical output encompassed 215 cantatas, preludes, fugues, motets, passions, chorales, sacred music, chamber music, and concertos. He was renowned for his mastery of counterpoint and his ability to develop musical motifs in his compositions. One of Bach's famous works, *The Well-Tempered Clavier*, consists of two books with 24 preludes and fugues each, written in every major and minor key. Our "Prelude in C Major" is part of this collection.

Bach was fruitful and prolific in both his compositions as well as his offspring. He married twice, with his first marriage to his second cousin, Maria Barbara Bach, resulting in seven children, although three died at a young age. Bach further experienced a tragic loss when

he returned from a trip one day only to find that Maria, 35 years old and healthy at the time, had unexpectedly died and had been buried in his absence. The cause of her death is not documented. The following year, Bach met Anna Magdalena, a talented soprano whom he married. They had a total of 13 children, but only six survived into adulthood. Anna Magdalena, a talented musician herself, together with her husband, was able to run a household with servants and students in which music supported their entire family.

☐ Play a C Major Scale with both hands ascending and descending 5 times.

☐ Try playing the C Major arpeggio with both hands together:

Video link: *https://www.musicmousestudios.com/piano-instructional-videos*

Practice Exercises

☐ Practice Exercise #1 (Review) – Clap and count the rhythm below.

☐ Practice Exercise #2 (Review) – Clap and count the rhythm below.

Play the following exercises with the appropriate rhythm, fingering, and dynamics. Write down the letter notes if needed.

☐ Practice Exercise #3 – Notice the sharp starting on the second note.

Video link: https://www.musicmousestudios.com/piano-instructional-videosa

☐ Practice Exercise #4

☐ Practice Exercise #5 – Notice the sharp starting on the third note.

☐ Practice Exercise #6

☐ Practice Exercise #7

Practice Exercises

Play the following exercises with the appropriate rhythm, fingering, and dynamics. Write down the letters on top of the notes if needed.

Video link: *https://www.musicmousestudios.com/piano-instructional-videos*

☐ Practice Exercise #8

☐ Practice Exercise #9

☐ Practice Exercise #10

☐ Practice Exercise #11 – Play this with your left hand.

☐ Practice Exercise #12 – Play this with your left hand.

☐ Practice Exercise #13 – Play this with your left hand.

New Song: "Prelude in C Major" (Part 2)

☐ Write down all the letters above or below the music notes.

☐ Circle all the places where you play **p**.

☐ Circle all the places where you play **pp**.

☐ What measure(s) do you crescendo?

☐ What measure do you decrescendo?

☐ What sharp is in measure 10?

Remember, this sharp carries across the whole measure.

☐ What sharp is in measure 12?

Remember, this sharp carries across the whole measure.

Video link: https://www.musicmousestudios.com/piano-instructional-videos

- [ ] Clap and count the rhythm of the right hand. Notice how every single measure has the same rhythm.
- [ ] Clap and count the rhythm of the left hand. Notice how every single measure has the same rhythm.
- [ ] Finger the right hand on the table. Follow the fingering provided.
- [ ] Finger the left hand on the table. Follow the fingering provided.
- [ ] Finger the song with both hands on the table.
- [ ] Play this song slowly with your right hand first.
- [ ] Play this song slowly with your left hand.
- [ ] Play this song slowly with hands together.

Congratulations, you've completed Lesson 16!

"Never say never, because limits,
like fears, are often just an illusion."

—MICHAEL JORDAN

LESSON
17
G Major Glory

Let's explore G Major in its full glory!

A key signature is a series of sharps or flats displayed at the beginning of a piece of music, following the clef symbol. It indicates which black keys must be played consistently throughout the entire song. These sharps or flats apply to every measure, meaning that if, for instance, there is an F♯ in the key signature, every occurrence of the note F in the song will be played as F♯.

G Major Introduction

In the key signature of G Major, the note F is represented as F♯, as mentioned earlier. Here is how it appears when written on the staff.

Observe how F♯ is written on the top line F in the treble clef since the line notes in the treble clef are EGBDF ("Every Good Boy Does Fine"), with F being the top line note. Similarly, in the bass clef, we can find the F that we want to sharpen by remembering that the line notes from bottom to top are GBDFA ("Good Boys Do Fine Always").

When drawing the key signature, ensure that the middle portion of the sharp symbol is on the F line, similar to how you draw a circle for a whole note. Take a moment to draw the G Major key signature on the staff provided.

Now, let's locate F♯ on the piano. Begin by finding the note F, then move to the next black key to the right of it.

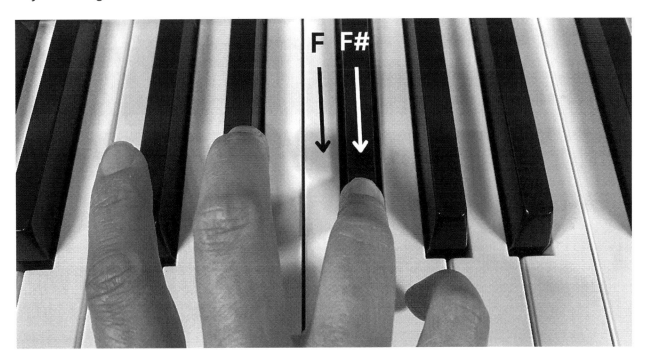

Video link: https://www.musicmousestudios.com/piano-instructional-videos

G Major Fingering

In today's lesson, we will focus on playing a G Major scale. As a reminder, a Major scale follows the pattern of:

whole step, whole step, half step,

whole step,

whole step, whole step, half step.

Applying this pattern to the starting note G, we get the notes G, A, B, C, D, E, F♯, and G, which is why the key signature of G Major contains one sharp, which is F♯.

The image above displays the notes of a G Major scale on the piano and the recommended fingering for the **right hand**. We start with the right thumb on G, then the index finger on A, the middle finger on B, cross under with the thumb to C, the index finger on D, the middle finger on E, the ring finger on F♯, and finally end with the pinky on G. When descending, follow the same order in reverse: start with the pinky on G, use the ring finger on F♯, middle finger on E, index finger on D, thumb on C, cross over with the middle finger on B, index finger on A, and finally, use the thumb on G.

For left hand fingering, refer to the visual below.

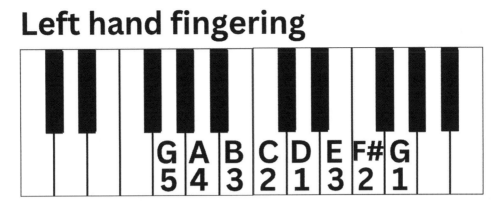

Left hand fingering

When ascending with the left hand, begin with the pinky on G, proceed to the ring finger on A, middle finger on B, the index finger on C, thumb on D, cross over with the middle finger to E, use the index finger for F♯, and finally, reach the top note G with the thumb. When descending, follow the reverse order: start with the thumb on G, move to the index finger on F♯, middle finger for E, cross under with the thumb to play D, continue with the index finger on C, the middle finger on B, the ring finger on A, and the pinky for G.

Warmup

☐ Play an ascending and descending G Major Scale with your right hand 5 times.

☐ Play an ascending and descending G Major Scale with your left hand 5 times.

☐ Play an ascending and descending G Major Scale with both hands together 5 times.

Video link: *https://www.musicmousestudios.com/piano-instructional-videos*

Playing Exercises

We will continue to learn Bach's "Prelude in C Major" today. Let's do a couple of playing exercises to help us reinforce the song!

Play the following exercises with the appropriate rhythm, fingering, and dynamics. Write down the letters on top of the notes if needed.

Video link: *https://www.musicmousestudios.com/piano-instructional-videos*

☐ Practice Exercise #1

☐ Practice Exercise #2 – Note the flat on the first note.

☐ Practice Exercise #3

☐ Practice Exercise #4 – Note the flat on the third note.

1 2 4   **1 2 4**

☐ Practice Exercise #5 – Observe the flat on the third note.

1 2 4   **1 2 4**

☐ Practice Exercise #6

1 2 3   **1 2 3**

☐ Practice Exercise #7

1 2 4   **1 2 4**

☐ Practice Exercise #8

1 2 4   **1 2 4**

☐ Practice Exercise #9

☐ Practice Exercise #10 – Use your left hand for this exercise.

☐ Practice Exercise #11 – Watch out for all the sharps and flats. Use your left hand for this exercise.

☐ Practice Exercise #12 – Use your left hand for this exercise.

New Song:
"Prelude in C Major" (Part 3)

DAY
162-165

☐ Write down all the letters above or below the music notes (this is optional).

☐ What measure(s) do you crescendo?

☐ What measure(s) do you decrescendo?

☐ What measure do you play *pp*?

☐ What flat is in measure 20? Remember that every time you see a B in this measure, it is flat.

☐ What sharps and flats do you see in measure 22? Remember, both the sharp and the flat carry across the full measure.

☐ What flats do you see in measures 23-24?

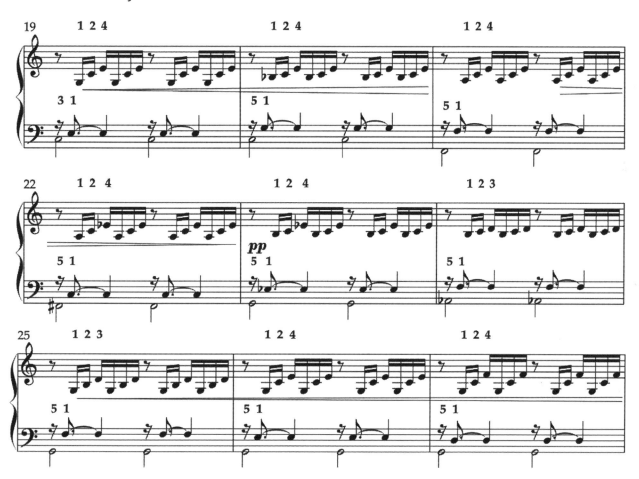

☐ Clap and count the rhythm of the right hand. Notice how every single measure has the same rhythm.

☐ Clap and count the rhythm of the left hand. Notice how every single measure has the same rhythm.

☐ Finger the right hand on the table. Follow the fingering provided.

☐ Finger the left hand on the table. Follow the fingering provided.

☐ Finger the song with both hands on the table.

☐ Play this song slowly with your right hand first.

☐ Play this song slowly with your left hand.

☐ Play this song slowly with hands together.

Video link: *https://www.musicmousestudios.com/piano-instructional-videos*

Congratulations, you've completed Lesson 17!

"It does not matter how slowly you
go as long as you do not stop."

—CONFUCIUS

LESSON
18
Expressive Techniques

Music is not music without emotion! In this lesson, we will explore
diverse chords and notes that infuse our music with flavor. Additionally,
we will investigate various tempo modifiers that enhance expression
and evoke a sense of drama in our musical performances!

Warmup Review

☐ Play an ascending and descending C Major Scale with both hands 5 times.

☐ Play an ascending and descending G Major Scale with both hands 5 times.

Dominant 7th Chord

Today, we're going to be learning what a dominant 7th chord is. Previously, we discussed the dominant chord as being built on a triad with the 1, 3, and 5 notes on a scale. A dominant 7th chord takes this triad and adds another 3rd on top, specifically the 7th note of the scale (hence the name "Dominant 7th"). Therefore, a dominant 7th chord consists of the 1st, 3rd, 5th, and 7th notes of the scale.

This 7th is lowered by a half step (making it a minor 7th instead of a major 7th chord). Taking a C dominant 7th chord as an example, the natural 7th note of C Major is B. However, a C Dominant 7th chord will lower that B by a half step to a B♭, with the notes of the C Dominant 7th chord being C, E, G, B♭. Dominant 7ths can help add more flavor to a piece of music and creates an even stronger desire to resolve to the tonic with the flat 7th.

Let's consider another example with the G dominant 7th chord, consisting of the notes G, B, D, and F (the F is lowered by a half step from F♯).

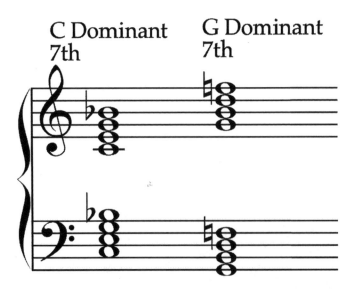

Video link: *https://www.musicmousestudios.com/piano-instructional-videos*

Like other triads, dominant 7th chords can also be played in different inversions and may have missing notes, which is typical. However, the 7th note will always be included to imply that it is a dominant 7th chord.

Although we will not cover the specific inversions of dominant 7th chords at this time, it is important to note that they exist and function similarly to the inversions of triads. Any of the notes in a dominant 7th chord can be the bottom note, and the notes within the chord can be arranged in different orders.

Naturals

In the G dominant 7th chord, you might notice a symbol preceding the F. This symbol is called a **natural** sign, which instructs the performer to play the regular white note instead of any sharps or flats played previously or indicated by the key signature.

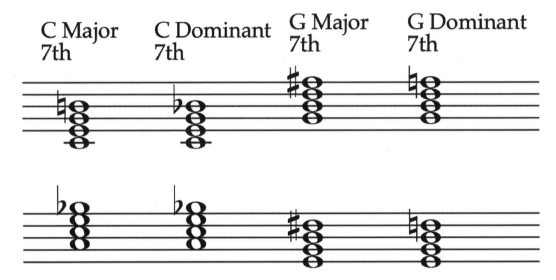

In the case of the G dominant 7th chord, instead of playing the F♯ typically found in G Major (as shown in the regular G Major 7th chord below), we play an F♮ in the G Dominant 7th chord. Similarly, in the C dominant 7th chord, rather than playing the usual B♮ in a C Major 7th chord, we lower it by a half step to a B♭.

Ritardando

Ritardando is a tempo marking in music that instructs the performer to gradually slow down the pace. This often occurs at the end of the piece, section, or at the conclusion of a phrase to enhance the sense of drama and provide a sense of finality. In the song we're playing today, you will see the tempo marking "*poco rit.*" "Poco" in Italian means "little," and "rit." is an abbreviation for "ritardando." So "*poco rit.*" means to slow down a little bit.

Fermata

A **fermata** is a notation symbol that indicates that a note or a chord should be held longer than its written value.

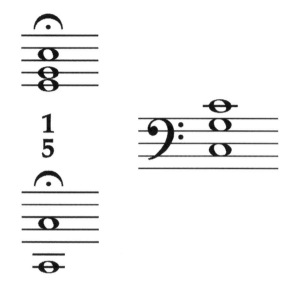

The performer has the freedom to determine the length of the pause. Like ritardando, fermatas are typically found at the end of a piece, phrase, or section to provide a sense of conclusion. There will be a fermata in the next music section we'll be playing. The fermata symbol resembles a bird's eye and is placed above the note or chord it affects.

Practice drawing a fermata on the bass clef C chord above.

Playing Exercises

We will be finishing up Bach's Prelude in C Major today! Let's do a couple of playing exercises to help us finish strong!

☐ Theory Exercise #1 – Look at the notes in the measure above. List out what the notes are.

☐ Theory Exercise #2 – If we're in the key of C Major? What chord does this make?

The notes G, B, and F imply a G Dominant 7th chord. Considering that this song is in C Major, a G Dominant 7th chord is fitting because G is the 5th, or dominant, in the C Major scale.

Play the following exercises with the appropriate rhythm, fingering, and dynamics. Write down the letters notes if needed.

Video link*: https://www.musicmousestudios.com/piano-instructional-videos*

☐ Practice Exercise #1

☐ Practice Exercise #2 – Pay attention to the sharp on the third note.

☐ Practice Exercise #3

☐ Practice Exercise #4

☐ Practice Exercise #5 – Pay attention to the flat on the second note.

Video link: https://www.musicmousestudios.com/piano-instructional-videos

☐ Practice Exercise #6 – Pay attention to the fourth finger movement. Play this slowly and follow the fingering provided.

☐ Practice Exercise #7 – Use your **right hand** for this exercise. Play this slowly and follow the fingering provided.

☐ Practice Exercise #8 – Use your **left hand** for this exercise.

☐ Practice Exercise #9 – Use your **left hand** for this exercise.

☐ Practice Exercise #10 – Use your **left hand** for this exercise.

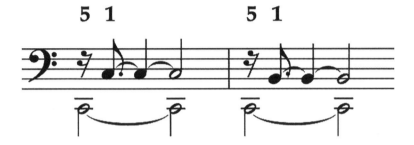

New Song: 'Prelude in C Major" (Part 4)

☐ Write down all the letters above or below the music notes (optional).

☐ What is the name of the chord in measure 28?

☐ What other measure do you see with a dominant 7th chord?

☐ What measure(s) do you crescendo?

☐ What measure(s) do you decrescendo?

☐ What measure do you play *f*?

☐ What measure do you play *p*?

☐ What flats and sharps are in measure 29? Remember that these carry throughout the measure.

- [ ] What sign do you see in measure 30?

- [ ] What flats do you see in measure 33? Remember that these flats persist throughout the measure.

- [ ] In measure 34, what clef is the right hand playing in? What clef is the left hand playing in?

Notice how they are both in the same clef since the notes that the right hand plays are very low and best notated with a bass clef rather than a treble clef.

- [ ] In measure 35, what note do you start to slow down playing a little bit on?

- [ ] What symbol do you see in the last measure in both the right and left hands?

- [ ] Clap and count the rhythm of the right hand. Notice how every measure has the same rhythm except for the last one.

- [ ] Clap and count the rhythm of the left hand. Notice how every measure has the same rhythm except for the last one.

- [ ] Finger the right hand on the table. Follow the fingering provided.

- [ ] Finger the left hand on the table. Follow the fingering provided.

- [ ] Finger the song with both hands on the table.

- [ ] Play this song slowly with your right hand first.

- [ ] Play this song slowly with your left hand.

- [ ] Play this song slowly with hands together.

Video link: *https://www.musicmousestudios.com/piano-instructional-videos*

Congratulations, you've completed Lesson 18!

"Character consists of what you do
on the third and fourth tries."

—JAMES A. MICHENER

LESSON
19
Pedal Magic

Now… for the icing on the cake… we will learn the art of using the pedal to seamlessly blend all the notes together, resulting in a serene musical landscape!

Warmup Review

☐ Play a C Major Scale with both hands ascending and descending 5 times.

☐ Play a G Major Scale with both hands ascending and descending 5 times.

☐ Play a C Major Arpeggio with both hands.

☐ Play a G Major Arpeggio with both hands. Notice how in the right hand, the notes are an octave lower.

☐ Play an F Major Arpeggio with both hands. Notice how in the right hand, the notes are an octave lower.

Video link*: https://www.musicmousestudios.com/piano-instructional-videos*

Chord Progressions Review

1 What key is the chord progression below in?

2 Label the Roman Numerals for the chord progression above.

3 What key is the chord progression below in?

4 Label the Roman Numerals for the chord progression above.

5 What key is the chord progression below in?

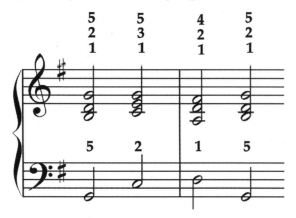

6 Label the Roman Numerals for the chord progression above.

7 What key is the chord progression below in?

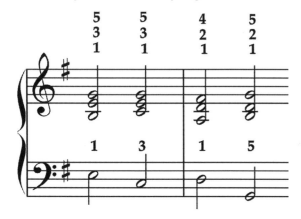

8 Label the Roman Numerals for the chord progression above.

Answers

1 C Major

2

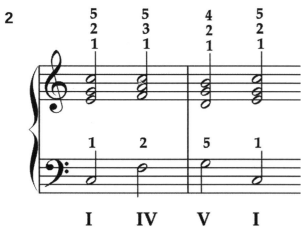

I   IV   V   I

3 C Major

4

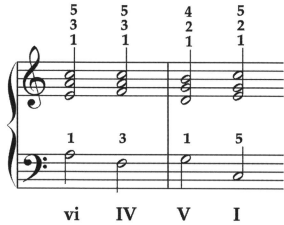

vi   IV   V   I

5 G Major

6

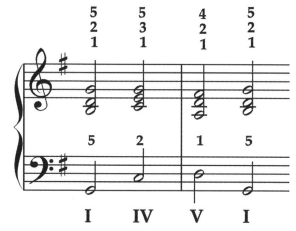

I   IV   V   I

7 G Major

8

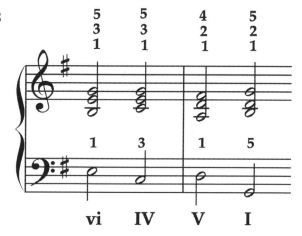

vi   IV   V   I

Playing Exercises

Try playing the chord progressions from the previous exercises and use the fingering provided.

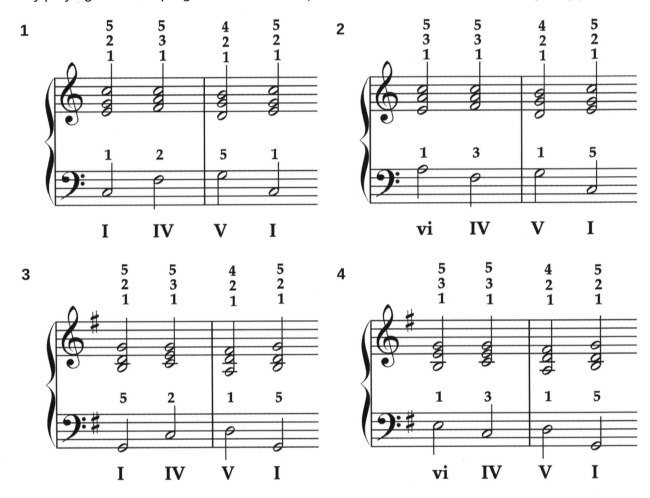

Video link: *https://www.musicmousestudios.com/piano-instructional-videos*

Choose one of the chord progressions above and play the bass clef notes with your left hand. With your right hand, play any of the notes in a C Major scale in any order to make up your own melody!

Video link: *https://www.musicmousestudios.com/piano-instructional-videos*

Sustain Pedal

The sustain pedal, located at the bottom of the piano or keyboard, is used to sustain the notes played on the piano, ensuring a smooth and connected sound.

On an acoustic piano, the pedal on the right is the sustain pedal. When using a sustain pedal, make sure that the heel of your foot is placed firmly on the ground and that your toe is facing upward.

On a keyboard, there is generally just one electric pedal, but the same rule of thumb applies – ensure that the heel of your foot is placed firmly on the ground and your toe is facing upward, and then press down.

The timing of applying the sustain pedal is crucial for achieving that smooth and connected sound in your piano playing. The pedal should be pressed immediately **after** changing a chord or measure, ensuring that it catches the note while you're still holding the keys down. It's important to *slightly delay your foot* pressing the pedal after your fingers press the keys. This creates an overlap, allowing the sound to sustain either through the notes held down by your fingers or by the sustain pedal operated by your foot.

Let's apply the pedal to the "Prelude in C Major" piece that we've been practicing. Try pushing down the sustain pedal right *after* the 16th rest in the left hand (so, for example, we should be pushing the pedal down right when we play that left hand E in the first measure). The second time you should press the pedal down would be after the 16th rest on beat 3, on that second E in the left hand.

Prelude in C Major
from The Well-Tempered Clavier

Johann Sebastian Bach

Try out the sustain pedal on that first row of 3 measures. Starting with measure 1, play the middle C with your left hand. Then immediately, as you're playing the E that follows, push down the sustain pedal and hold it through until **right after** you play that middle C again with your left hand on beat 1 of measure 2 and then lift the sustain pedal quickly and then push it down again so that the sustain pedal lands right at the same time with the D. Then you will do the same thing and hold the sustain pedal down through the first beat of measure 3 (through the B below middle C) and right after playing that note, lift the sustain pedal quickly and put it back down again on that D that follows the B after beat 1 on the "a." Essentially, the sustain pedal will always lag behind that first note held down by your fingers ever so slightly but then the pedal will be down and sustaining that note when your fingers lift up from it and go to the second note. It's this overlap that helps to create that long, sustained line. Refer to the video to hear it in action.

Video link: *https://www.musicmousestudios.com/piano-instructional-videos*

Let's apply the sustain pedal to the rest of Bach's "Prelude in C Major."

New Song: "Prelude in C Major" – Putting It All Together

Prelude in C Major

from *The Well-Tempered Clavier*

Johann Sebastian Bach

Now you know all of the sections that make up this piece. We are going to put it all together now!

☐ Play this song slowly with your right hand first.

☐ Play this song slowly with your left hand.

☐ Play this song slowly with hands together.

☐ Add the sustain pedal.

☐ Practice until you feel confident with it!

☐ Perform this song for someone you know!

Video link*: https://www.musicmousestudios.com/piano-instructional-videos*

Congratulations, you've completed Lesson 19!

"You've got to get up every morning with determination if you're going to go to bed with satisfaction."

—GEORGE LORIMER

LESSON
20
The Art of
Articulation

Punctuation, emphasis, pacing, melodic motion – we will tackle these
and more as we master the art of articulation in the next lesson!

DAY 186   Warmup Review

- ☐ Play an ascending and descending C Major Scale with both hands 5 times.
- ☐ Play an ascending and descending G Major Scale with both hands 5 times.
- ☐ Play a C Major Arpeggio with both hands.

- ☐ Play a G Major Arpeggio with both hands.

- ☐ Play an F Major Arpeggio with both hands.

The order of sharps is a specific sequence of sharps used to determine the key signature. The order is as follows: F♯, C♯, G♯, D♯, A♯, E♯, B♯. How do we apply the order of sharps?

If a key signature has 1 sharp, it will be F♯, as it is the first sharp in the order. If a key signature has 2 sharps, it will be F♯ and C♯, the first two sharps in the sequence. Similarly, for 3 sharps, the key signature will be F♯, C♯, and G♯, following the first three sharps in the order, and so on.

Now let's take that previous example of a key signature having 3 sharps F♯ C♯ G♯. How do we determine the key signature from these 3 sharps? The rule of thumb here is to **take the last sharp (G♯ in this case) and raise it up by a half step** to determine the key that you're in. So a half step up from G♯ is A Major. Therefore, the key of A Major has F♯ C♯ G♯ in it.

Let's Practice!

See if you can answer the questions below:

1   If a key signature has 2 sharps, what are the sharps?

2   What key would we be in?

3   If a key signature has 4 sharps, what are the sharps?

4   What key would we be in?

5   If a key signature has 5 sharps, what are the sharps?

6   What key would we be in?

7   If a key signature has 7 sharps, what are the sharps?

8   What key would we be in?

Answers

1   F♯ C♯

2   D Major

3   F♯ C♯ G♯ D♯

4   E Major

5   F♯ C♯ G♯ D♯ A♯

6   B Major

7   F♯ C♯ G♯ D♯ A♯ E♯ B♯

8   C♯ Major

DAY 188

Staccato vs. Legato

Staccato is an articulation marking used to indicate which notes should be played in a short and detached manner. It is represented by a small dot placed above the notes. **Legato** is the opposite of staccato and refers to playing notes smoothly and connected without noticeable breaks between them. In some cases, legato is indicated by a slur marking, but often it is the default way of playing unless specified otherwise.

Play the exercises below. The first note of each measure should be played legato, followed by 2 staccato notes on G (played first by the thumb and then by the index finger the second time around).

Video link: https://www.musicmousestudios.com/piano-instructional-videos

Parallel Motion

Parallel motion refers to the simultaneous movement of two hands playing notes in the same direction. We observe parallel motion in our warm-ups as we play ascending and descending scales.

In the example below, notice how this simultaneous upward movement of both hands demonstrates parallel motion.

Allegretto

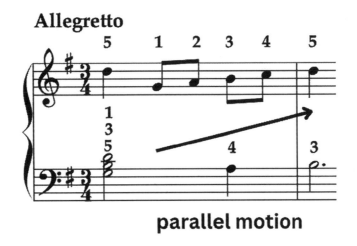

parallel motion

☐ Play the above exercise with your right hand alone.

☐ Play the above exercise with your left hand alone.

☐ Play the above exercise with both hands. Feel the parallel motion in your hands as they move in the same direction.

Video link: *https://www.musicmousestudios.com/piano-instructional-videos*

Contrary Motion

On the contrary, **contrary motion** is the opposite of parallel motion, where the hands play and move in opposite directions. In the example below, the left hand notes move to the left while the right hand notes simultaneously move to the right, exemplifying contrary motion.

☐ Play the above exercise with right hand alone.

☐ Play the above exercise with left hand alone.

☐ Play the above exercise with both hands. Feel the contrary motion in your hands as they move in the same direction.

contrary motion

Video link: *https://www.musicmousestudios.com/piano-instructional-videos*

New Song: "Minuet 3 in G Major" (Part 1)

Today we will start a new song called "Minuet 3" in G Major by Christian Petzgold! We will be learning this song throughout the next several lessons. The tempo marking is "Allegretto," which indicates a moderately fast pace. The term "Allegretto" contains the Italian diminutive "-etto," meaning "little," suggesting a slightly slower tempo than the standard "Allegro."

Minuet 3
in G Major

Christian Petzgold
Minuet from the "Notebook for Anna Magedalena Bach"

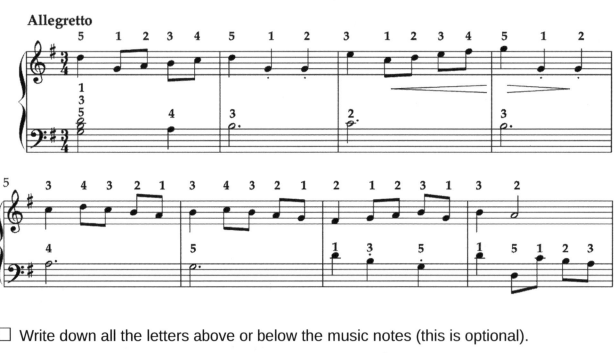

☐ Write down all the letters above or below the music notes (this is optional).

☐ How many sharps are in this song, and what is the key signature?

☐ How many beats are there in a measure?

☐ What measure do you crescendo?

☐ What measure do you decrescendo?

☐ In measure 1, what interval do we see in the right hand from beat 1 to beat 2 (from D to G)?

☐ In measure 2, what interval do you see in the right hand from beat 1 to beat 2 (from D to G)?

- [ ] In measure 3, what interval do you see in the right hand from beat 1 to beat 2 (from E to C)?

- [ ] In measure 4, what interval do you see in the right hand from beat 1 to beat 2 (from G to G)?

- [ ] In measure 7, what intervals do you see in the left hand (from D to B, B to G)?

- [ ] In measure 8, what interval do you see in the left hand from beat 1 to 2 (from D to D)? What about from beat 2 to 2& (D to C)?

- [ ] Point to all the areas where there is stepwise motion (going up or down the scale by 2nds).

The melody in the right hand consists of a combination of leaps and steps. In measure 1, there is a 5th interval between the first and the second note (D to G). Then, we continue with stepwise motion up the scale until the second measure, where another 5th leap occurs from D to G. Moving to measure 3, the first beat starts with a downward leap of a 3rd, followed by an upward stepwise motion leading into the 4th measure. In measure 4, we encounter the largest leap yet of an octave down from G to G. The remaining section predominantly consists of stepwise motion for the right hand. In contrast, the left hand exhibits downward leaps in 3rds in the seventh measure and an octave leap below in the eighth measure.

- [ ] Circle all the staccato notes.

- [ ] Clap and count the rhythm of the right hand. Notice how the rhythm in measures 1-2 is the same as in measures 3-4. Measures 5, 6, and 7 also have the same rhythm.

- [ ] Clap and count the rhythm of the left hand. How many dotted half notes do you see? (There should be 5).

- [ ] Finger the right hand on the table. Follow the fingering provided in the song.

- [ ] Finger the left hand on the table. Follow the fingering provided in the song.

- [ ] Finger the song with both hands on the table.

- [ ] Play this song slowly with your right hand first.

- [ ] Play this song slowly with your left hand.

- [ ] Play this song slowly with hands together.

Video link: https://www.musicmousestudios.com/piano-instructional-videos

About Christian Petzold

Christian Petzold, a German composer and organist, lived from 1677 to 1733 and held the position of court chamber composer in 1709. While only a few of his works have survived, the "Minuet in G Major" we are currently learning is one of them. This piece was preserved in the *Notebook for Anna Magdalena Bach* (Anna Magdalena being the second wife of Johann Sebastian Bach).

Petzold's "Minuet in G Major" and his "Minuet in G Minor" are well-known pieces featured in the notebook. Initially, these compositions were mistakenly attributed to Anna's husband, J.S. Bach, until scholars corrected this in the 1970s. Petzgold was good-natured and well-regarded amongst his contemporaries.

☐ Perform "Prelude in C Major" for someone or share it with us on our website, www.musicmousestudios.com!

Congratulations, you've completed Lesson 20!

"What you get by achieving your goals is not as important as what you become by achieving your goals."

—ZIG ZIGLAR

LESSON
21
Form and Function

"What is not like the other?" is a common question we teach even kids to recognize. Determining where patterns exist in music is essential in developing efficient practice habits as well as understanding the form of a piece. We will dive more into this in the upcoming lesson!

Warmup Review

☐ Play a C Major Scale with both hands ascending and descending 5 times.

☐ Play a G Major Scale with both hands ascending and descending 5 times.

☐ Play a C Major Arpeggio with both hands.

☐ Play a G Major Arpeggio with both hands.

☐ Play an F Major Arpeggio with both hands.

We will learn the next section of Minuet 3 in G Major. Let's look at the section below and compare it to the section we learned last week.

New section

Last section

Minuet 3

in G Major

Christian Petzgold
Minuet from the "Notebook for Anna Magedalena Bach"

What do you notice? For starters, if we look at the **right hand**, it remains **mostly unchanged** throughout, except for the final two measures of each section. The left hand is also similar, with just the addition of some notes filled in here and there.

Referring to the previous section (measures 1-8) as **Section A**, we can label the subsequent section (measures 9-16) as **A'** since it closely resembles A but with slight variations.

It's essential to discern *where* the key differences are between the two sections, which in this case, is primarily found in their endings.

☐ What notes do you see in beats 2 and 3 of measure 8 (using both hands)?

We see the D, C, B, and A. The B is a leading note to A, so the core notes here are D, A, and C.

☐ What chord does D, A, and C imply?

If we put these notes into a chord made up of 3rds, we have D, F# (implied), A, and C. This makes a D dominant 7th chord.

☐ Since this piece ends with a V, what cadence is this?

This is called a half cadence, as we learned in previous lessons. Half cadences lack a sense of resolution, like a sentence ending with a question mark that prompts a subsequent response.

☐ Let's look at measure 15. What notes are in this measure?

We see the notes C, D, A, B, G, F#. If we remove the B and G passing tones, we are left with D, F#, A, and C, a D dominant 7th chord.

☐ Let's look at measure 16. What notes are in this measure?

It only has one note, and that is G. This implies a G Major chord, which is also the tonic.

☐ Knowing this, what cadence does the A' section end on (from dominant 7th to tonic)?

The A' section concludes with an authentic cadence, bringing a sense of resolution by ending on the tonic chord. This provides a definitive answer to the question posed in the A section and creates a feeling of finality.

Playing Exercises

Let's practice some legato and staccato exercises before digging into the next section of the piece. Play the exercises below!

Video link: *https://www.musicmousestudios.com/piano-instructional-videos*

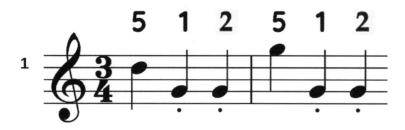

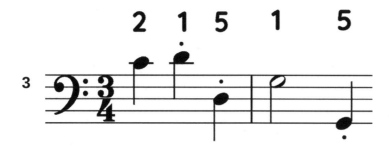

New Song:
"Minuet 3 in G Major" (Part 2)

DAY
197-200

☐ Write down all the letters above or below the music notes (this is optional).

☐ How many sharps are in this song, and what is the key signature?

☐ How many beats are there in a measure?

☐ Circle all the staccato notes.

☐ Label the Authentic Cadence at the end of this section with the Roman Numerals (V7 I) under the proper notes.

☐ Clap and count the rhythm of the right hand.

☐ Clap and count the rhythm of the left hand.

☐ Finger the right hand on the table. Follow the fingering provided in the song.

☐ Finger the left hand on the table. Follow the fingering provided in the song.

☐ Finger the song with both hands on the table.

☐ Play this song slowly with your right hand first.

☐ Play this song slowly with your left hand.

☐ Play this song slowly with hands together.

Video link: *https://www.musicmousestudios.com/piano-instructional-videos*

Congratulations, you've completed Lesson 21!

"The only time you should ever look back is to see how far you've come."

—BTS, SOUTH KOREAN BAND

LESSON
22
Flavor of Flats

Join us as we traverse into the land of flats and explore F Major!

☐ Play a C Major Scale with both hands ascending and descending 5 times.

☐ Play a G Major Scale with both hands ascending and descending 5 times.

☐ As a review, practice playing the following chord progressions:

I   IV   V   I

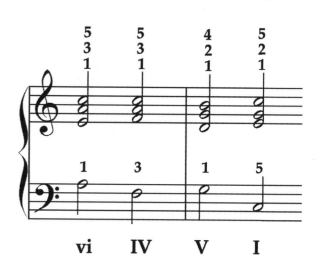

vi   IV   V   I

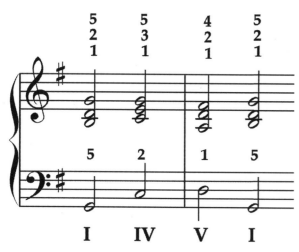

I   IV   V   I

vi   IV   V   I

The Order of Flats serves a similar function to the Order of Sharps - the number of flats present help define the key signature. However, there is one difference to note: the rule does not apply to the first flat, which is B♭. **If a key signature contains only B♭, the key is in F Major.**

The Order of Flats is as follows: B♭, E♭, A♭, D♭, G♭, C♭, F♭. An easy mnemonic to remember this order is the word "BEAD" followed by "GCF" (Greatest Common Factor). Another delightful acronym that can serve as a memory aid is: "Blueberry Eating Always Did Get Cows Fat."

Based on the flats present, **we look at the second-to-last flat to determine the key signature**. For example, if there are 2 flats, B♭ and E♭, we find the second-to-last flat (B♭) and determine that the key is B♭ Major. If there are 3 flats (B♭, E♭, A♭), the second-to-last flat (E♭) indicates that the key is E♭ Major. Similarly, if there are 4 flats (B♭, E♭, A♭, D♭), the second-to-last flat (A♭) reveals that the key is A♭ Major. This method can be used to determine the key signature for the remaining flats in the Order of Flats.

Let's Practice!

See if you can answer the questions below:

1   If a key signature has 2 flats, what are the flats?

2   What key would we be in?

3   If a key signature has 4 flats, what are the flats?

4   What key would we be in?

5   If a key signature has 5 flats, what are the flats?

6   What key would we be in?

7   If a key signature has 7 flats, what are the sharps?

8   What key would we be in?

Answers

1   B♭ E♭

2   B♭ Major

3   B♭ E♭ A♭ D♭

4   A♭ Major

5   B♭ E♭ A♭ D♭ G♭

6   D♭ Major

7   B♭ E♭ A♭ D♭ G♭ C♭ F♭

8   C♭ Major

F Major Introduction

As a refresher, if a key signature has one flat displayed after the clef, that flat is B♭, and the song is in F Major. This means that every time you see a B in a measure, you will play B♭ instead. This is what an F Major key signature looks like on the staff.

Notice how the B♭ is written on the middle line B in the treble clef. If you remember from previous lessons, the line notes from the bottom to top are EGBDF ("Every Good Boy Does Fine"), with the middle line note being B. This is the B that you want to lower and put a flat on when writing the key signature for F Major.

Similarly, in the bass clef, the line notes from the bottom up are GBDFA ("Good Boys Do Fine Always"). The B line note here is also the one we want to lower in our key signature from B to B♭. For the B♭ in both the treble and bass clef, we want to draw the flat so that the middle portion is on the B line, similar to how you draw a circle for a whole note on line notes.

☐ Draw the F Major key signature above on the staff to your right.

Now, how do we find B♭ on the piano? First, we find B, then we move down to the black note to the left of it.

Playing an F Major Scale

Today, we will be learning how to play an F Major scale. As a refresher, a Major scale consists of the half note whole note pattern -

whole whole half
whole
whole whole half

Applying this to the starting note F, we can derive the F Major scale: F, G, A, B♭, C, D, E, F, which is how we conclude that the key signature of F Major consists of 1 flat, and that is B♭.

The image below represents the F Major scale with the corresponding fingerings. In the right hand, we play F with our thumb, G with our index finger, A with our middle finger, and B♭ with our **ring finger**. Then, we cross under with the thumb to play C, followed by D with the index finger, E with the middle finger, and F with the ring finger. When descending, we follow the same pattern but in reverse order. Note that the fingerings differ slightly from C and G Major. Instead of playing fingers 1, 2, 3 and then crossing over with the right thumb, we instead play 1, 2, 3, 4, and then cross the thumb under, due to the B♭.

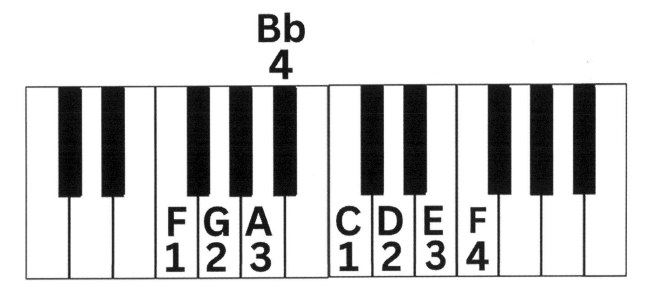

F Major - Right hand fingering

For the left hand, the fingering remains the same as in C and G Major. Please refer to the visual below. With the left hand, we ascend the scale starting with the pinky on F, followed by G with the ring finger, A with the middle finger, B♭ with the index finger, and C with the thumb. Then, we cross over with the middle finger to play D, followed by E with the index finger and F with the thumb. When descending, we start with F on the thumb, go down to E with the index finger, then D with the middle finger, cross under with the thumb to C, and continue descending with B♭ on the index finger, A on the middle finger, G on the ring finger, and finally F on the pinky.

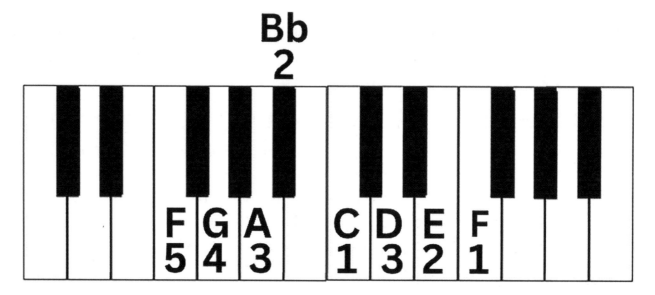

F Major - Left hand fingering

☐ Play an F Major Scale with your right hand ascending and descending 5 times.

☐ Play an F Major Scale with your left hand ascending and descending 5 times.

☐ Play an F Major Scale with both hands ascending and descending 5 times.

Video link: https://www.musicmousestudios.com/piano-instructional-videos

Playing Exercises

Let's practice some legato and staccato exercises before digging into the next section of the piece. Play the exercises below with the fingerings provided!

Video link: https://www.musicmousestudios.com/piano-instructional-videos

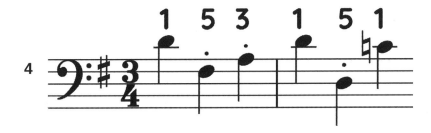

Motifs

Similar to the A sections, we observe a combination of leaps and stepwise motion in this next section of the song. Look at the right hand in beats 2 and 3 in measures 17, 18, and 19. Notice the recurring pattern in the melody, where two 2nd intervals are followed by a leap of a 3rd.

Look at the patterns below -

Despite starting on different notes in each measure, this recurring pattern serves as a melodic anchor for this section, and we call this pattern a **motif**, which is a short musical idea or theme that repeats in different variations throughout a song.

In addition to the motif, if we examine the notes that precede each motif on beat 1 of measures 17, 18, and 19, we find the notes B, A, and G. These descending notes create their own mini melody that accompanies the motif and moves it along the descending scale.

Moving forward, measures 21-22 feature an ascending and then descending scale, followed by leaps in measures 23-24 to conclude this section. This section looks decently different from the previous A sections, so we will call this section B.

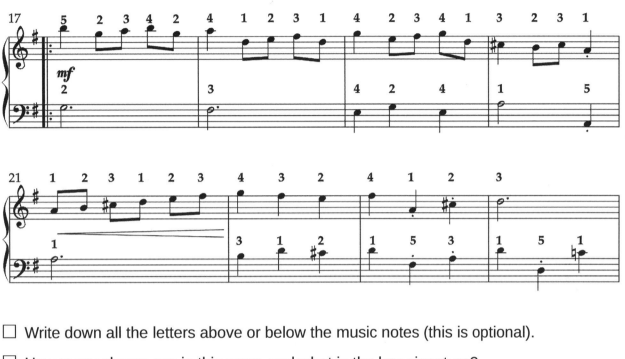

☐ Write down all the letters above or below the music notes (this is optional).

☐ How many sharps are in this song, and what is the key signature?

☐ How many beats are there in a measure?

☐ What dynamic marking do you start with in measure 17, and what does that mean?

☐ What measure do you crescendo?

☐ Circle all the staccato notes.

☐ Clap and count the rhythm of the right hand. Notice how the rhythm in measures 17-19 is all the same.

☐ Clap and count the rhythm of the left hand. How many dotted half notes do you see?

(There should be 3).

Video link: *https://www.musicmousestudios.com/piano-instructional-videos*

☐ What sharp do you see in measures 20-23?

☐ What symbol do you see in measure 24 in front of the left hand C?

☐ Finger the right hand on the table. Follow the fingering provided in the song.

☐ Finger the left hand on the table. Follow the fingering provided in the song.

☐ Finger the song with both hands on the table.

☐ Play this song slowly with your right hand first.

☐ Play this song slowly with your left hand.

☐ Play this song slowly with hands together.

Congratulations, you've completed Lesson 22!

"All the adversity I've had in my life, all my troubles and obstacles, have strengthened me… You may not realize it when it happens, but a kick in the teeth may be the best thing in the world for you."

—WALT DISNEY

LESSON
23
The Grand Finale

Your remarkable progress as a pianist is truly commendable, showcasing tremendous growth. We are almost at the finish line! Let's channel that determination and drive toward a resounding grand finale!!

DAY 211 Warmup Review

☐ Play a C Major Scale with both hands ascending and descending 5 times.

☐ Play a G Major Scale with both hands ascending and descending 5 times.

☐ Play an F Major Scale with both hands ascending and descending 5 times.

☐ As a review, practice playing the following chord progressions:

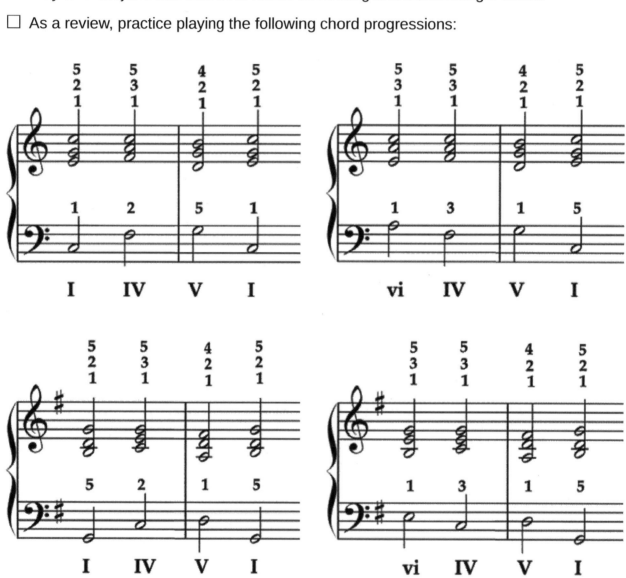

Let's practice some legato and staccato exercises before digging into the next section of the piece. Play the exercises below with the fingering provided!

Video link: *https://www.musicmousestudios.com/piano-instructional-videos*

B, B'

In today's lesson, we will cover the final section of this song. Let's compare the previous B section with the new one.

New section

Old section

While this second B section is not as similar to the first B section as the A and A', their melodic structures bear a decent amount of resemblance.

In this new B' section, we observe the usage of a motif on beats 2 and 3 of measures 25-26 in the right hand. Another similarity is found in the last 4 measures of the section, where it once again has a rising and falling scale that is followed by leaps to bring the section to a close.

☐ Look at measure 24. What notes are in that measure, and what chord does that make?

The notes are D and C natural. The implied chord here is a D Dominant 7th chord with D, (F# implied), (A implied), and C natural.

☐ What cadence does section B end on in measure 24?

Because it ends on a V chord, it is a Half Cadence.

Once again, this is similar to the A section ending in a Half Cadence. Let's examine what kind of cadence the B' section ends with.

☐ Look at measure 31, beat 3. What notes do you see there, and what chord does that make?

We see the notes D and F#. This creates a D Major chord (D, F#, and the A is implied). We know that the D is the 5th note in the G Major scale, so D is the dominant.

☐ Look at measure 32. What notes do you see there, and what chord does that make?

The notes we see are G, B, and D. This makes none other than a G Major chord, the tonic in a G Major scale.

☐ What cadence does B' end with?

Knowing that it ends with V I, this is an authentic cadence.

Similar to the transition from A to A', going from a half cadence at the end of B to an authentic cadence in B', this again creates tension and resolution to the tonic.

New Song:
"Minuet 3 in G Major" (Part 4)

☐ Write down all the letters above or below the music notes (this is optional).

☐ How many sharps are in this song, and what is the key signature?

☐ How many beats are there in a measure?

☐ Circle all the staccato notes.

☐ Label the Authentic Cadence at the end of this section with the Roman Numerals (V I) under the proper notes.

☐ What dynamic do you start playing the piece at?

☐ What measure do you crescendo in?

☐ Clap and count the rhythm of the right hand.

☐ Clap and count the rhythm of the left hand.

☐ Finger the right hand on the table. Follow the fingering provided.

☐ Finger the left hand on the table. Follow the fingering provided.

☐ Finger the song with both hands on the table.

☐ Play this song slowly with your right hand first.

☐ Play this song slowly with your left hand.

☐ Play this song slowly with hands together.

Video link: https://www.musicmousestudios.com/piano-instructional-videos

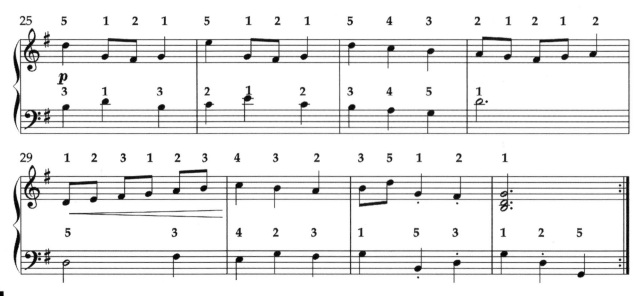

Warmup Review

☐ Play a C Major Scale with both hands ascending and descending 3 times.

☐ Play a G Major Scale with both hands ascending and descending 3 times.

☐ Play an F Major Scale with both hands ascending and descending 3 times.

☐ Play a C Major Arpeggio with both hands.

☐ Play a G Major Arpeggio with both hands.

☐ Play an F Major Arpeggio with both hands.

New Song: Minuet 3 in G Major by Christian Petzgold (Part 5)

Minuet 3

in G Major

Christian Petzgold
Minuet from the "Notebook for Anna Magedalena Bach"

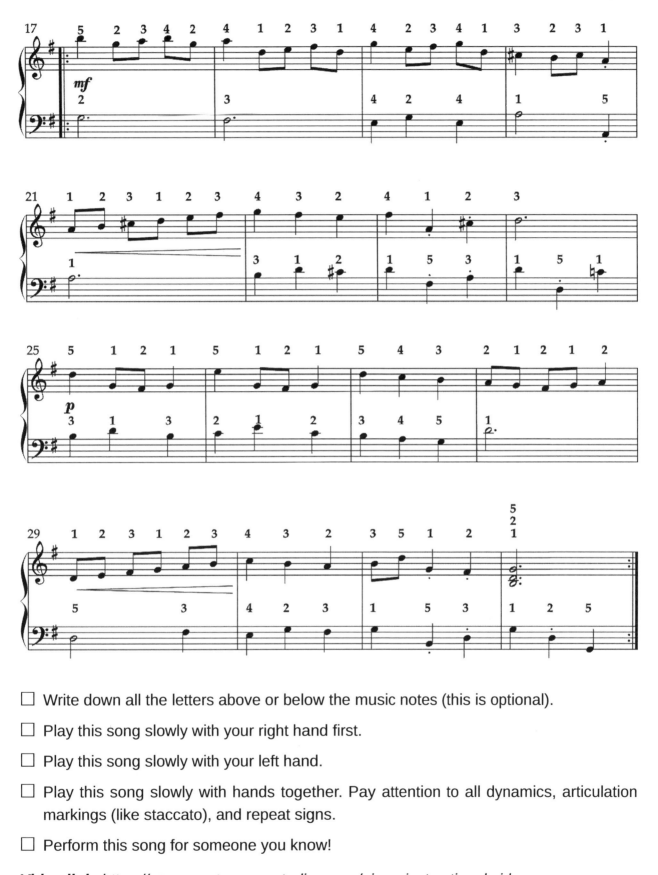

☐ Write down all the letters above or below the music notes (this is optional).

☐ Play this song slowly with your right hand first.

☐ Play this song slowly with your left hand.

☐ Play this song slowly with hands together. Pay attention to all dynamics, articulation markings (like staccato), and repeat signs.

☐ Perform this song for someone you know!

Video link*: https://www.musicmousestudios.com/piano-instructional-videos*

Congratulations, you've completed Lesson 23!

"You are never too old to set another
goal or to dream a new dream."

—AUDREY HEPBURN

Performance (OPTIONAL)

Practice all of the songs from Book 1 and Book 2 and perform them for someone or share it with us on our website, www.musicmousestudios.com!

☐ Mary Had a Little Lamb

☐ Down the River

☐ Oh When the Saints Go Marching In

☐ Twinkle, Twinkle Little Star

☐ The Amazing Twinkle, Twinkle Little Star

☐ Ode to Joy

☐ Go Tell Aunt Rhody

☐ Amazing Grace

☐ Brahms Lullaby

☐ Danny Boy

☐ Prelude in C Major

☐ Minuet 3

CERTIFICATE
OF AWARD

presented to :

Congratulations! You have graduated from Book 2 -
Your Golden Ears: First Piano Lessons for Adult Beginners!

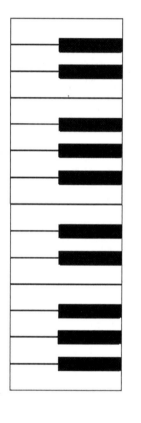

Andrea Chang

Founder of
Music Mouse Studios

Date

Leave A 1-Click Review!

I would be incredibly thankful if you could just take 60 seconds to write a brief review on Amazon, even if it's just a few sentences.

Customer reviews

★★★★★ 5 out of 5

2 global ratings

5 star	████████████	100%
4 star		0%
3 star		0%
2 star		0%
1 star		0%

⌄ How customer reviews and ratings work

Review this product

Share your thoughts with other customers

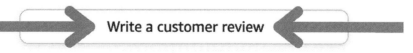

Write a customer review

Conclusion – Beyond the Last Note

Congratulations, you've achieved it! Completing this course was no small accomplishment, but your perseverance has paid off splendidly! Throughout this journey, we've delved into crucial subjects, from honing our finger dexterity through warm-ups, songs, and scales, to exploring music theory at a deeper level through harmonic analysis of cadences and interval movements. You've also learned to elevate your artistry by infusing your playing with expressive techniques, such as dynamics, articulation, and the sustain pedal. You've even conquered intricate compositions like Bach's "Prelude in C Major" and Petzgold's "Minuet 3 in G Major." Furthermore, you've dived into the realm of artistic improvisation, truly creating your own musical path!

As you reach the conclusion of this book, bear in mind that your journey as a pianist is just commencing! Continuing to learn, practice, and challenge yourself is paramount. IDon't be discouraged by challenges; instead, see them as stepping stones to growth and improvement. You now possess the tools and knowledge to apply what you have learned, and this book will serve as a valuable resource you can always refer back to.

Put into practice all that you have learned and persistently pursue excellence in your piano playing. Embrace the opportunity to apply your knowledge, honing your skills with dedication and a commitment to continuous improvement. We believe in your ability to achieve greatness in your musical endeavors! Share your progress with us, inspire others, and continue to pursue your musical dreams with passion and determination!!

If you have found value in this book, we kindly ask for your support. Please consider leaving a positive review on Amazon and subscribing to our YouTube channel, where you will find more valuable content and piano lessons! Visit us at https://www.youtube.com/@homeschoolingwithandrea.

For personalized assistance, additional resources, and support, we invite you to explore our website, www.musicmousestudios.com. You will find a wealth of information to aid you on your musical journey.

And don't forget about your free gift!
To receive this exclusive download of additional sheet music and songs, simply visit https://www.musicmousestudios.com/contact and include the text "SHEET MUSIC" in your message.

We have thoroughly enjoyed being a part of your piano journey so far, and we are excited to continue supporting you as you grow and excel as a pianist. The best is yet to come!

Keep playing, keep learning, and keep reaching for the stars!

References

Wikipedia contributors. (2023f). Johannes Brahms. *Wikipedia*. https://en.wikipedia.org/wiki/
Johannes_Brahms

Pew, D. (2018). Classical Music's Most Tragically Romantic Love Triangle — Timpanogos
Symphony Orchestra. *Timpanogos Symphony Orchestra*. https://thetso.org/blog/
love-triangle

Songfacts. (n.d.). *Cradle Song by Johannes Brahms - Songfacts*. Songfacts. https://www.
songfacts.com/facts/johannes-brahms/cradle-song

Wikipedia contributors. (2022). Christian Petzold (composer). *Wikipedia*. https://en.wikipedia.org/
wiki/Christian_Petzold_(composer)

Christian Petzold: German Composer from The Baroque Era. (n.d.). Galaxy Music Notes. https://
galaxymusicnotes.com/pages/about-christian-petzold

Wikipedia contributors. (2023f). Johann Sebastian Bach. *Wikipedia*. https://en.wikipedia.org/wiki/
Johann_Sebastian_Bach

Simplifying Theory. (2020, June 17). *Supertonic, mediant, submediant and
leading-tone | Simplifying Theory*. https://www.simplifyingtheory.com/
supertonic-mediant-submediant-and-leading-tone/

200+ Motivational Quotes To Inspire and Win 2023. (2022, December 1). Shopify. https://www.
shopify.com/blog/motivational-quotes

Liles, M. (2023, March 9). Stay Motivated When the Going Gets Tough Thanks to These 100
Quotes About Not Giving Up. Parade: Entertainment, Recipes, Health, Life, Holidays.
https://parade.com/980122/marynliles/not-giving-up-quotes/

117 Never Give Up Quotes (+ My 5 Favorite Tips to Help You Keep Going). (2022, April 25). The
Positivity Blog. https://www.positivityblog.com/never-give-up-quotes/

Edinburgh, K. (2023). 55 Uplifting Quotes to Encourage Making
Progress. Exam Study Expert. https://examstudyexpert.com/
progress-quotes/#quotes-to-help-you-get-a-new-perspective-on-your-progress

You Can Do It Quotes. (n.d.). BrainyQuote. https://www.brainyquote.com/topics/
you-can-do-it-quotes

Made in the USA
Las Vegas, NV
11 November 2024